Treasured Turtles:
Life in a Shell

Dive Into the World of Turtles With Fun Facts, Amazing Photos, and Everything You Need to Know!

CHARLOTTE GIBBS

© **Copyright 2024 - All rights reserved.**

The content contained within this book may not be reproduced, duplicated, or transmitted without direct written permission from the author or the publisher.

Under no circumstances will any blame or legal responsibility be held against the publisher or author for any damages, reparation, or monetary loss due to the information contained within this book, either directly or indirectly.

Legal Notice:
This book is copyright-protected. It is only for personal use. You cannot amend, distribute, sell, use, quote, or paraphrase any part of the content within this book without the consent of the author or publisher.

Disclaimer Notice:
Please note the information contained within this document is for educational and entertainment purposes only. Every effort has been executed to present accurate, up-to-date, reliable, and complete information. No warranties of any kind are declared or implied. Readers acknowledge that the author is not engaged in rendering legal, financial, medical, or professional advice. The content within this book has been derived from various sources. Please consult a licensed professional before attempting any techniques outlined in this book.

By reading this document, the reader agrees that under no circumstances is the author responsible for any losses, direct or indirect, that are incurred as a result of the use of the information contained within this document, including, but not limited to, errors, omissions, or inaccuracies.

Table of Contents

Introduction—Let's Talk Turtles!   5

CHAPTER 1
Types and Species of Turtles   7
Tortoises: Slow and Steady Shell Rockers!   8
Freshwater turtles: Aquatic Wonders of the River Realm!   9
Sea Turtles: Ocean Navigators of the Deep Blue!   9

CHAPTER 2
Turtle Anatomy   13
Turtle Shell: The Cool Armor Story!   14
Turtle Legs: The Amazing Adaptations of Nature   15
Turtle Trot: Exploring Their Slow Moves   16
Turtle Senses: Feeling Their Surroundings   16

CHAPTER 3
Turtle Habitat   19
Freshwater Turtles: Water-Loving Turtles   20
Land Tortoises: Desert Dwellers   22
Sea Turtles: Splashing in the Ocean   22
Safeguarding Their Special Places   23

CHAPTER 4
Turtle Diet   25
Finding Food: How They Find Yummy Treats   27

CHAPTER 5
Turtle Behavior 29

Turtle Behavior: Eating, Sunbathing, Digging, and more adventures! 30
Turtle Nursery: Where Turtles Begin 31
Turtle Migration: Amazing Journeys 33

CHAPTER 6
Life Cycle of Turtles 37

Turtle eggs: A Fun Eggstravaganza 38
Hatching: Egg-citing Day! 39
Growing Up and Starting the Cycle Again! 39

CHAPTER 7
Threats to Turtles & Conservation Efforts 43

Awesome Things People Are Doing to Help 45

Conclusion 49

Introduction—Let's Talk Turtles!

Welcome to Turtles for Kids!

Yep, we're going to be talking a lot about turtles. And why not? Turtles are cute and clever and carry a little home on their backs. They also make excellent pets for many people around the world. So, what's not to love? But that's just the beginning. We're going to talk about many more interesting and fascinating things about turtles with some cool facts to impress your friends with. Or at least Mom and Dad.

Now, turtles are amazing creatures that have been around for millions of years, yes, millions! Around 230 million years, if you really want to know! I bet you're wondering, "Have turtles been around since the time of the dinosaurs?" Well, the answer is YES! Hard to believe, right? And they've survived this long because they're so cool. You see, their bodies don't need a lot of energy to live because, one, they are super tough little things, and two, they move slowly and purposely. That saves energy and that saving of energy has helped them survive tough times like when there's little food around. And turtles live in the water, so that protects them from any disasters happening on land such as meteors and volcanic eruptions that were said to cause the extinction of the dinosaurs. Turtles and other creatures living in the water, or creatures that could burrow like turtles, were able to hide away from all the drama!

Isn't that super interesting? Well, we've only just begun. In this book, you're going to learn about all the different types of turtles, about their unique bodies (they're pretty funny creatures when you think about it!), where they live and how they've adapted to their environment, what they eat, their curious behavior, their life cycle from egg to adult, and lastly the threats to turtles and the conservations efforts to help them.

Are you ready? Let's jump in!

CHAPTER 1
Types and Species of Turtles

Terrific Turtle Types and Super Species!

You might be surprised to learn that there are so many different types of turtles—from tiny ones that can fit in your hand to huge ones that might be bigger than you!

There are land turtles, freshwater turtles, and sea turtles, with over 350 different species of turtles in the world! Let's first take a look at land turtles, otherwise known as tortoises!

TORTOISES: SLOW AND STEADY SHELL ROCKERS!

These are hardy guys! Tortoises can live in deserts, forests, grasslands, and other harsh places. Some live in tropical areas like the Sri Lankan and Indian tortoise called the Indian Star—named for the star pattern on their backs. They make great pets, these types, and can live for hundreds of years! Imagine having a pet that could live longer than your great-grandparents! Some tortoises like to burrow and this has helped them survive all those millions of years. We can't skip over the magnificent **Giant Galapagos tortoise** that can even go without water for a whole year due to their ability to store water! These turtles are not only huge and live long, they are gentle, sweet creatures, too. These two guys you see on the picture are two Giant Galapagos tortoises! Huge, right?

Two Galápagos giants on the move!

FRESHWATER TURTLES: AQUATIC WONDERS OF THE RIVER REALM!

Freshwater turtles live in many different environments, from ponds to lakes to streams and even in bogs! Its soft shell is mostly used to protect it from predators—a handy thing to have! Some popular types are:

- **The Painted Turtle from North America:** this turtle shows off some awesome colors. It's just like they're walking around with a rainbow on their back!
- **The Yangtze giant softshell turtle:** this rare and endangered turtle has a pig-like snout! Can you picture a turtle with a little piggy nose? How funny! This is the largest freshwater turtle.

Freshwater turtles love to sunbathe on rocks and logs, soaking up the warm sunshine. Sometimes, they stack on top of each other like a turtle tower!

SEA TURTLES: OCEAN NAVIGATORS OF THE DEEP BLUE!

Sea turtles live in the sea—of course! They live in almost every ocean in the world, with some swimming remarkable distances to feed and others preferring to stay close to home. These are two remarkable sea turtles:

- The **Leatherback Turtle** stands out for the unbelievable distances it can swim. It can swim over 10,000 miles a year between foraging and nesting grounds—that's like swimming across the world!
- Then we have the **Loggerhead Turtle**, the most abundant species of turtle in America. Their name comes from their large heads that support their jaw muscles. They need this strong jaw to crush their food—such as clams and sea urchins.

Another amazing thing about sea turtles is they can travel so, so far, but then still manage to find their way back to where they were born and lay their eggs on the very same beach! One thing to note here is unlike their land and freshwater friends; they cannot pop their little heads back inside to hide from danger. However, to make up for it, they have a very strong front flipper that helps them speed through the water and dodge any danger!

Next time you encounter a turtle, take a good look! You might be observing a slow-and-steady shell-dweller, a vibrant painted turtle gliding through the water, or perhaps even a majestic sea turtle—a true marvel of the ocean depths! Isn't the shelled world fascinating?

A colorful sea turtle gliding through a coral reef adventure!

Bonus Facts!

1. Turtles come in a variety of sizes and shapes; they can be as small as a few inches long or as large as over 1,000 pounds!
2. With a maximum weight of 2,000 pounds, the leatherback sea turtle is the largest type of turtle.
3. All continents, with the exception of Antarctica, are home to turtle populations.
4. Since turtles have cold blood, their temperature changes according to the environment they are in.
5. The speckled padloper tortoise, which only reaches a length of about 3 inches, is the tiniest turtle.

CHAPTER 2
Turtle Anatomy

The Totally Awesome Turtle Body!

You must admit, turtles are pretty unique looking! They have a long neck, cute stumpy legs, and on their backs, a sort of home they can duck back into whenever they like. Maybe they want to hide from a predator, or maybe they have a loud buddy who just doesn't stop talking, and they need to pop inside their shell for a bit of quiet time.

TURTLE SHELL: THE COOL ARMOR STORY!

Check out this Indian star tortoise—what a cool pattern, right?

Interestingly, their shell, called a 'carapace,' is made of keratin—the same material as our skin and nails! This shell is attached to their bodies, so they never leave their shells but rather grow with the same shell. It's like carrying your house around and never having to worry about moving!

It is shaped like a dome so that if they happen to get flipped over onto their backs, they can more easily roll themselves back over. I'm guessing this is the same with beetles! I'll let you learn about beetles some other time!

The bottom part of the shell is called the 'plastron'. The shell, as we know, is used for protection but also buoyancy—its design and materials help it float, swim, and move more easily through the water. No wonder they make it look easy!

TURTLE LEGS: THE AMAZING ADAPTATIONS OF NATURE

Now, let's take a look at their legs.

- **Super Swimmer Legs:** Freshwater turtles' legs are really flexible, helping them swim through the water. They also have little bits of webbing between their toes and small claws. Cute!
- **Digging and Climbing:** They also have extra skin on their legs to help them move about, dig, and climb over logs for nesting and more.
- **Scaly Shields:** Tortoises have thick scales covering their legs, and you know what? When they pop inside their shells for protection, they use these strong, scaly legs as a shield to block the entrance to their shell. Cool, hey?
- **Elephant Feet:** Tortoises have claws too. Their feet are super hardy because they live in some harsh places at times, and if you take a look, you'll notice they look a lot like elephant feet! They need these super strong feet because they spend a lot of time walking long distances and exploring, and those larger tortoises need to carry quite a bit of weight. They sure are hardy!

- **Flipper Power:** And, of course, we can't talk about legs when it comes to sea turtles because they have flippers, like little fins, that help propel them through the ocean. They spend most of their time in the water and only come on land to lay eggs – and because they are moving through sand, their flippers are enough to get them around.

TURTLE TROT: EXPLORING THEIR SLOW MOVES

While on the topic of movement, you may be wondering—why are turtles and tortoises so slow? Well, there's a few reasons. Firstly, they don't need to be fast in order to catch their food. Being herbivores (eating plants only), they can potter about nibbling a little grass here and a little flower there. Other animals, such as rabbits, need to move very fast to escape being caught by foxes. No one really bothers turtles and tortoises because they have that awesome hard shell that protects them. They simply pop inside, and no one gets to them. Sea turtles, as mentioned earlier, can't go inside their shells, but they can swim fast to escape. Being slow helps them conserve energy and helps them avoid injuries. And you know what? If they moved faster, they'd need to eat more to fuel that energy to move faster. Slow and steady wins the race!

TURTLE SENSES: FEELING THEIR SURROUNDINGS

Turtles and tortoises have some pretty amazing senses. Let's explore:

- **Super Sniffers:** Turtles and tortoises have a very good sense of smell—so they can sniff out yummy food.
- **Keen Eyesight:** Freshwater turtles' and tortoises' sight is excellent on land and in water.
- **Special Ears:** Turtles don't have ears and only 'hear' at a very low frequency through vibrations in the air, land, and water that alert them to things like predators.

- **Magnetic Sense:** For sea turtles in the water, their eyesight is excellent but quite bad out of the water, and that makes sense. Also, sea turtles have a special sense whereby they are able to navigate the long distances they travel. They are able to sense the sun and magnetic fields that give them a sense of where they are in the world and have a sort of internal magnetic map that helps them to find their old nesting and feeding grounds that are sometimes thousands of miles apart! How cool is that?

Bonus Facts!

1. Squirtle is a Water-type Pokémon with a cool shell that helps it swim fast and shoot powerful jets of water. It's friendly and brave, always ready to protect its friends and win battles!

2. Did you know that The Teenage Mutant Ninja Turtles' names—Leonardo, Michelangelo, Donatello, and Raphael—are all inspired by Renaissance artists?

3. Green sea turtles are named for the greenish color of their fat, not their shells.

4. At up to 550 pounds, the Aldabra giant tortoise is among the heaviest of all turtle species.

5. Turtles symbolize longevity, patience, and wisdom.

CHAPTER 3
Turtle Habitat

Discover Their Cozy Homes!

It's interesting how turtles live in such varied environments. Let's take a closer look at a few of them.

FRESHWATER TURTLES: WATER-LOVING TURTLES

Behold the amazing diamondback terrapin in all its glory!

First up, let's look at freshwater turtles that live in lakes, rivers, marshlands, streams, and little ponds in someone's yard if they are pets!

- **Webbed Wonders:** They have webbed feet, so they can swim, but they still have solid legs to walk around, burrow, and dig.
- **Cold-Blooded Cuties:** Freshwater turtles are like reptiles—cold-blooded, with temperatures matching their environment. Being tough fellows, the

average turtle lives for around 20 years, but as we know, some can live to over one hundred or even two hundred years!

- **Springtime Sprinters:** Freshwater turtles become more active in spring when their lake, stream, or pond becomes warmer. That makes sense! They like this habitat with shallow water and soft mud at the bottom.

- **Mud Walkers:** Some turtles that are not the best swimmers even like to walk along the bottom of the mud, which is easier for them.

- **Land Lovers:** Turtles that live in the environment still need to come out onto land to lay eggs.

- **Hibernation Heroes:** When the water gets too cold, turtles like to hibernate in the water, burying themselves in the mud, sand, and pebbles until the water warms up. They remain dormant, slowing their metabolism right down and saving up all their energy and oxygen. It's like a long, cozy nap in the mud. Clever!

A beautiful leopard tortoise exploring South Africa's desert landscape.

LAND TORTOISES: DESERT DWELLERS

- **Rocky Roamers:** Desert tortoises have hardy feet that allow them to clamber over their rocky and dusty habitat.

- Cactus Crunchers: There is not much vegetation, so they eat what they can when they see it, including cactuses. Yum! Spiky but satisfying!

- Cool Burrowers: When it's hot or too cold, they crawl under low bushes or rocks and burrow into the sand for shelter.

- Sunny Sunbakers: They do love to sunbake in sunny areas.

- Estivation Experts: When it is very hot and dry, animals enter a state called estivation, where they are inactive and conserve water and energy.

- **Slow and Steady:** That slow walk also helps them conserve energy in the desert. They can last a very long time without water, getting the water they need only from plants. Talk about a survival trick!

SEA TURTLES: SPLASHING IN THE OCEAN

Then, we have sea turtles who spend most of their time underwater in the ocean.

- **Shallow Swimmers:** They tend to like shallow, clean areas like coastal waters, bays, seagrass beds, mangroves, lagoons, estuaries, and the ocean too—which particularly refers to the Leatherback Turtle that has the ability to dive deeply.

- **Reef Roamers:** They will stick to areas where there are also places to hide such as in coral reefs.

- **Tropical Travelers:** Sea turtles prefer warmer waters in tropical areas (we don't blame them!) and where there is lots of food around. Who wouldn't love a tropical paradise?

SAFEGUARDING THEIR SPECIAL PLACES

Speaking of clean areas—it is so very important that we help to keep our oceans and waterways clean for not only our turtles but all aquatic creatures. For example, turtles can get caught up in netting that's used to wrap our vegetables—which is why we should avoid such packaging of our food, and if we do come across such netting, it's best to cut it up finely before putting it into the trash. Many plastics that end up in our oceans and waterways harm turtles, such as plastic straws—so always choose paper straws!

Pollution can harm turtles' food sources and the nesting areas that are vital for a healthy turtle population.

Areas known to be nesting places for turtles must be protected and managed carefully. Creating special protected areas is also a great way to protect these beautiful creatures, such as their nesting grounds, feeding areas, and migration routes.

We must all aim to protect the natural habitats of turtles and tortoises because if we don't, we'll see a decline in their populations (many are already endangered), a disruption to the food chain (many are predators and prey with many animals relying on them for food), problems with marine and coastal ecosystems (turtles eat particular plants that if not eaten can grow out of control), and a loss of biodiversity—which means turtles help with the moving around of nutrients and can change the balance of the ecosystem.

Bonus Facts!

1. Some turtles have a very weird looking appearance. Have you seen the mata mata turtle? It has a flat, wide head and a long neck.

2. The leatherback sea turtle can dive deeper than any other sea turtle. It reaches depths of over 3,000 feet!

3. There's a type of turtle that can live both in freshwater and slightly salty (brackish) water. This group is called terrapin.

4. There's an animal that has the word turtle in its name, but it's not a turtle! It's a member of the doves and pigeons' family: the turtle dove!

5. The red-eared slider turtle is a popular pet turtle known for its vibrant red stripe behind its eyes.

CHAPTER 4
Turtle Diet

Turtles Treats: What's on Their Menu?

We know that turtles eat plants and grass, but what else? Turtles are like little vacuum cleaners of the wild! They are scavengers and eat a variety of things, such as water plants like duckweed, insects like beetles, dragonfly larvae, small fish, small frogs or tadpoles, snails or clams, and even dead animals they might come across. Pets or other turtles may also eat fruit or veggies if they fall into the water or they are fed it by us humans.

Tortoise Tastes: Tortoises prefer leafy greens, veggies, wild plants, flowers, cacti, grasses, and hay. One particular tortoise I know of just loves bananas! Tortoises have also been known to eat some non-food items—like bones, soil, feathers, hair, eggshells, and even... poop! Can you believe it? They might even munch on things you'd never think of as food!

Plastic Predicaments: All kinds of turtles can eat plastic thinking that it is something else, so again, be careful with disposing of your trash. A floating plastic bag might look like a tasty jellyfish to a sea turtle.

Coin Crunchers: Some turtles live in ponds where people throw coins in for good luck. You know the ones? Well, it's not so lucky for the turtles because they sometimes eat these coins by mistake! Imagine thinking you're getting a yummy snack, but it's actually a shiny coin. Ouch!

Ocean Appetites: Sea turtles eat sea grasses, algae, jellyfish, crabs, and fish, to name a few. They have quite the seafood buffet out there in the ocean!

FINDING FOOD: HOW THEY FIND YUMMY TREATS

Super Sniffers: But how do they get this food? Tortoises will use their sense of sight and smell and forage as they potter along. They also have the ability to remember where some yummy food is located and head back there again for another nibble! Talk about having a built-in GPS for snacks! They have a strong, beak-like mouth that helps them chew their sometimes tough food.

Freshwater Food Finders: Freshwater turtles also use their sense of smell and sight to locate their food and sometimes use the currents in the water to help bring the food their way. Some turtles lie in wait for food to come right by their snapping mouths (the snapping turtle!). They can also remember previous good food spots. Imagine waiting for dinner to just float by your front door!

Seafood Seekers: Sea turtles find their food also through smell, sight, and memory as they forage. They have very strong mouths that can crush food with hard shells. Their jaws are like powerful nutcrackers, perfect for their ocean treats!

From munching on leafy greens to snapping up a jellyfish, turtles know how to treat themselves to a delicious meal.

Bonus Facts!

1. Some cultures believe that turtles carry the world on their back or symbolize the Earth itself.//
2. The ancient Greeks and Romans believed that turtles were symbols of fertility and rebirth.
3. Franklin the Turtle is a friendly character from books and TV who first showed up in 1986, and he loves learning new things and having fun adventures with his friends!
4. Have you heard of the pancake tortoise? It has a super flat shell that lets it slip into tiny, snug spots to hide from hungry predators. This unique adaptation makes it look almost like a pancake!
5. You can figure out how old a turtle is by counting the rings on its shell, just like counting the rings on a tree!

CHAPTER 5
Turtle Behavior

Too-Cute Turtle Behavior

We've touched on turtle behavior, but let's dive in a little deeper!

TURTLE BEHAVIOR: EATING, SUNBATHING, DIGGING, AND MORE ADVENTURES!

So, let's start with tortoises. They love to forage slowly, looking for food. They take their time, enjoying each tasty bite as they wander. They also love to sunbathe—but why? Well, they are cold-blooded animals, like lizards, and need to warm their bodies in the sunshine, not to get a golden tan! They are active during the day, so they need the sun to warm them up and give them the energy for all that foraging. The sun also provides them with many necessary vitamins, just like we need vitamin D. It also helps them digest food… Interesting! Freshwater turtles also like to sunbathe for all the same reasons. And guess what! Sea turtles also sunbathe—on the beach, of course!

Tortoises and turtles love to dig for various reasons, such as to lay eggs, burrow, hide from predators, or escape very hot or very cold weather. On the flip side, sea turtles need to dig in order to lay their eggs in the sand.

Have you seen a turtle just floating in the water? They might be 'soaking'. They do this to hydrate their shell—to soak it up with water if it becomes too dry, and this behavior is more common with tortoises that live in the desert. They must come across a lovely oasis of water and dive in for a nice long soak before heading off to forage again.

What else do turtles do?

- **Rest and Relaxation:** They rest, often inside their shells. It's like having a cozy little house with you all the time!

- **Hiss and Grunt:** They use sounds to hiss or grunt during mating or if in tussles with other turtles! Who knew turtles could be so noisy?
- **Head Bobbing Fun:** How's this? When turtles are trying to impress a mate or are curious about a new object, they bob their heads—that must be a cute and funny sight!
- **Stress Rocking:** If stressed, a turtle may rock back and forth.
- **Lunging for Love:** When they are shown food they love, they can lunge forward with their mouths already open, ready for that delicious bite. This is another cute sight to behold.
- **Turtle Towers:** Some smaller turtles like to stack on top of each other to get to their destinations, which is also fun to watch.

Look at this painted turtle basking in the warm sun's rays!

TURTLE NURSERY: WHERE TURTLES BEGIN

Now, let's explore a super important behavior of turtles—nesting.

Female tortoises choose the perfect spot—where there's loose sand or soil and with enough sunshine (for all that sunbaking). They use their strong legs and claws to burrow and dig out a cozy area. Next, she will lay her eggs one at a time before covering up the nest. The nest must be covered well so that sneaky predators don't come and steal her eggs. For some animals, they make a delicious treat! After she's done, she goes back to whatever she likes to do—sunbaking and foraging, I'd say. It can take weeks or months for the eggs to hatch, depending on the species of tortoise, and when they hatch, these little guys are totally on their own, with no mom around to find food for them or provide protection. Thankfully, they have an inbuilt sense of how to behave, like hiding under rocks for protection.

Freshwater turtles leave the water to create their nests in a very similar way to tortoises, but digging a hole in a safe, protected area with their back legs. They are smart and usually choose to dig their nest after it's been raining so that the soil is softer and easier to push around.

Sea turtles create nests in a very similar way, emerging from the ocean and creating a nest up on the sand dunes. They usually make their nests at night when it is cooler and to avoid predators. The super interesting thing about sea turtles is their ability to remember (after often traveling very far away) the exact beach where they were born and create their nest there, too. And this is another reason why they build their nests at night. They use the moon and stars to help them navigate to that special spot and also that inbuilt map we mentioned earlier. How amazing!

Instead of using their back legs, sea turtles use their strong flippers, which do the job well. Then the hatchlings emerge; they race to the sea as quickly as their little flippers can take them because predators everywhere are trying to grab one for a snack! Only one in one thousand hatchlings make it to adulthood. It's a tough world out there for these guys, and that's even more reason that we need to help protect them.

It's a beautiful sight to see so many baby turtles make their way to the ocean, and there are many places around the world where you can see this sight for yourself.

TURTLE MIGRATION: AMAZING JOURNEYS

Another unique behavior is their migration skills. Turtles and tortoises can move quite long distances according to the seasons from one area to another and not just for a change of scenery! They have specific reasons for this behavior.

- **Food Finders:** They can move because they are searching for more or better food.
- **Nesting Necessities:** They move to find the perfect nesting site to lay their eggs.
- **Water Seekers:** In search of water, they may remember where pools and lakes from after a rainy season.
- **Temperature Travelers:** For a change in temperature, perhaps move to a cooler or warmer area.
- **Habitat Heroes:** If their habitat is threatened by building in their area or clearing land and vegetation, turtles may move to new areas. Scientists have observed this, and many efforts are being made to protect turtles' habitats and migratory paths and routes, which are so important to them for all the reasons above.

Protecting Their Pathways:

Some habitats are being restored to encourage turtles and tortoises to come back, and others are being protected from humans entering and disturbing their environment. Let's help them travel safely!

Sea Turtle Navigation:

Sea turtles migrate for all the same reasons, but they also have a built-in map that helps them navigate super-long distances. They use geomagnetic field lines, waves, currents, and the positions of the sun, moon, and stars. They are true ocean navigators.

Bonus Facts!

1. There's a special turtle that glows in the dark, how fun! It's known as the spotter turtle, its spots look like they're glowing under certain lights.

2. Do you know who Yertle the Turle is? It's a turtle king from Dr. Seuss's book "Yertle the Turtle and Other Stories". He tries to stack other turtles to make himself the tallest, but ends up learning a valuable lesson about humility.

3. Some places have a traditional event that involves turtles: turtle racing! It's a slow and steady race, but very exciting.

4. Sports mascots are a big thing in the United States. The University of Maryland has a famous sports mascot named "Testudo," and it's a terrapin turtle!

5. In some parts of the world, people train turtles to "surf." It's a fun trick and quite impressive!

CHAPTER 6
Life Cycle of Turtles

Turtle Tales: From Hatchlings to Heroes!

TURTLE EGGS: A FUN EGGSTRAVAGANZA

Okay, so you know all about nesting and how the mom lays the eggs in the nest, and how they can take from weeks to months to hatch. The eggs are formed very similarly to tortoises, freshwater turtles, and sea turtles. The number of eggs laid varies but can be up to one hundred! Next, they need to incubate, whereby the temperature needs to be just right for the eggs to develop into tiny turtles. The time and temperature vary. A special type of gas exchange occurs, and the nest needs to be at the right depth for this to happen properly. The temperature during incubation is super important and as mentioned at the very start of the book, will decide whether there will be more male or female babies born!

HATCHING: EGG-CITING DAY!

Just before they hatch, the tiny turtle absorbs the egg sac, which gives it lots of nutrients to help it become strong for the next stage. It's like having a snack before starting a big adventure! When the turtle is ready to come out, it wiggles about, causing the shell to break. Then, it's free! The little turtles hatch, and then they're on their own. They have now entered the juvenile stage. The race to the water or ocean is on, and it becomes survival of the fittest!

This stage is all about adapting to whatever habitat they've found themselves in. It might be a desert, river, ocean, or a little pond in someone's yard! They need to be able to find food successfully, escape predators (get super good at popping their head back in and pretending to be a rock!), burrow from heat or cold temperatures, and become experts at soaking up the sun (or water if they're in a desert) and move about to new habitats if they need.

GROWING UP AND STARTING THE CYCLE AGAIN!

The time it takes to become a mature adult turtle varies among species. Most freshwater turtles and tortoises can mate at around 5-10 years, but some can take 15-20 years. It all depends on the species and environment.

Friendship Finders: Turtles are social creatures so these juveniles will seek out other turtle friends where they feel more protected and where they can learn from each other. Safety in numbers makes for a fun turtle gang!

Learning and Growing: Eventually, they will be looking for a mate. The journey from baby turtle to adult is filled with learning and exploring!

- **Patience Pays Off:** Sea turtles take a lot longer to mature, with the Green Turtles, for example, taking from 20 to 50 years! Now, once they are mature, and usually around springtime, they are on the hunt to find a mate to produce more baby turtles.

- **Romantic Rituals:** Sea turtles have a funny way of attracting a mate. They like to nuzzle their new mate or gently bite the back or her rear flippers! Tortoises are a little different and make a bellowing sound, bob their heads, and nip her front legs, otherwise known as 'love bites.' Cute!

- **Freshwater Flirting:** Some freshwater turtles flutter their claws in the female's face and gently caress their face, releasing pheromones, a special scent to attract her. Imagine giving someone a gentle tickle to say, "I like you!" These are just a few examples of the different mating styles.

- **Double Duty:** After mating, the female turtle's next stage in the life cycle is going off to lay her eggs. She does this sometimes twice per year.

And then, the life cycle starts all over again!

Bonus Facts!

1. You've heard of the phrase "Slow and Steady Wins the Race", right? It comes from a famous fable called "The Tortoise and the Hare." The moral of the story is that consistent (and maybe slow) effort and persistence are more important than speed.

2. Two Russian tortoises were among the first animals sent into space by NASA.

3. Turtle's footprints can provide important information about their size, species, and even the conditions of their nesting sites.

4. The word "turtle" comes from the French word "tortue," which was inspired by the Latin word "tartaruchus," meaning "of the underworld."

5. Some turtles can breathe through their butts! The ability, called cloacal respiration, helps them get oxygen while they're underwater or hibernating.

CHAPTER 7
Threats to Turtles & Conservation Efforts

Save the Turtles: Dangers They Face and How We Can Help!

There are a lot of different turtle species as you've already learned. However, some of them are endangered, meaning that their lives and habitats are under threat. As discussed briefly already this could be for various reasons.

Their environment could be polluted with chemicals, plastics, or other harmful substances whereby it has leaked into their waterways or the ocean. Their habitat may have been destroyed by logging, land clearing, or natural disasters, or have become uninhabitable due to climate change where the water has become too warm to live in or other such changes to the climate that are affecting their particular environment. They may also be under threat from a predator. All these factors can make the survival of some species come under threat. The Giant Galapagos tortoise, for example, is endangered, and this is because sailors were hunting, and their habitat was becoming smaller. Conservationists are working hard to protect these beautiful creatures.

There are some sea turtles also under threat such as the Hawksbill Turtle. This particular turtle has various threats to its survival. Sadly, many people have captured this turtle in order to use its beautiful shell for jewelry and other purposes, which has led to its population decreasing. It is also under threat of losing some of its habitat from climate change affecting the coral reefs where it lives and also from being accidentally captured in big fishing trawlers.

While it is indeed sad and worrying that these gorgeous turtles and tortoises are under threat, the good news is some people are working hard to save and protect them.

AWESOME THINGS PEOPLE ARE DOING TO HELP

Some things people are doing are, as mentioned earlier, protecting nesting sites so they are not disturbed and raising awareness about the plight of some species and this helps people do the right thing when disposing of their trash. Raising awareness also leads to raising money, and that money goes to all of these efforts to protect certain areas, clean up the ocean, and more. Conservationists are also working to restore turtle habitats that were destroyed to encourage more turtles to come back and increase their population again, and there are some awesome breeding programs going on where they are breeding turtles safely, so they have a better chance at survival without all those predators around.

Another way to help the turtles is by teaching local communities better fishing practices to avoid turtles being caught in nets and to leave nesting grounds undisturbed. Also, all of the people working to stop and minimize climate change is another way to help turtles be able to remain in their comfortable habitats and not have to risk migrating to new unfamiliar areas.

But what can **you** do to help?

Here are lots of things you can do! Check them out!

- **Become a Turtle Hero!** If you happen to live near a turtle habitat, find out how you can get involved in volunteering to help protect that area, or if no one is protecting the area, you can start! You can write petitions or talk to your local government about starting ways to help this particular species of turtle.
- **Fundraiser Fun!** Start a fundraiser and raise money to donate to causes that are already helping protect and save endangered turtles. Every little bit can make a difference!
- **Say No to Shell Products!** Never buy anything made from turtle or tortoise shells.

- **Visit and Support!** Visit sea turtles where possible. It helps the turtles and their community.

- **Plastic Patrol!** Be sure to dispose of all plastics, especially balloons, netting, and straws, and tell your friends! Even better, try to avoid buying plastic items altogether! Use reusable bags to purchase fruits, veggies, and other items. There's really no need to use plastic bags, buy netted food, or use plastic straws at all. Many places now ban the use of these types of plastics but if you see them being used in your community, be sure to make an effort to have these banned by starting a petition or contacting local authorities.

- **Nighttime Ninja!** Turn off flashlights if on the beach at night. It can disturb hatchlings.

- **Beach Buddy!** Whenever you visit a beach, be aware of any nesting areas, and keep your distance.

- **Cleanup Crew!** Organize or join a beach, river, lake, or waterway cleanup. This way, you will help all turtles because most waterways also end up finding their way to the ocean.

- **Turtle Talk!** Use any opportunity to raise awareness and share information about turtles! Tell anyone who wants to listen about how cool they are, how they are endangered, and how they can help by doing all of the above!

Bonus Facts!

1. In ancient China, turtle shells were used to predict the future!
2. In some cultures around the world, turtle shells are lucky charms and are believed to bring good fortune and protection to whoever has them.
3. There's a famous, cool, laid-back sea turtle that you may know… Yes, it's Crush, a Green Sea Turtle that helps Marlin and Dory from "Finding Nemo" navigate the ocean. What a cool dude!
4. In places like Florida, there are special wildlife tunnels that were built to help turtles safely cross roads.
5. Some turtles can shed tears to clean their eyes and keep them healthy, just like how we use eye drops!

Conclusion

Turtles are ancient treasures. They're cute, interesting, clever, funny, and unique and are so crazily adapted to their environments that they've survived the dinosaurs! They help keep our environment healthy, and we owe it to them to look after their varied habitats so they don't one day become extinct. While they are super tough and have withstood many natural disasters, the biggest threat to these beautiful creatures are humans. We are the ones who are polluting and disturbing their delicate habitats, we are the ones buying plastics and throwing them out carelessly, and we are the ones who buy souvenirs made out of pretty shells. But we are also pretty smart, and we are the ones who can prevent endangered turtles from becoming extinct; we can help protect their habitats and restore some of their damaged environments, which will increase their population. So, keep learning and caring about our treasured turtles and spreading the word about how amazing they are. We think you're pretty amazing, too, for getting to the end of this book and becoming an expert on all things turtles!

Coloring Fun: Let's Paint Turtles!

SPECIAL BONUS!

Want These 2 Books For FREE?

 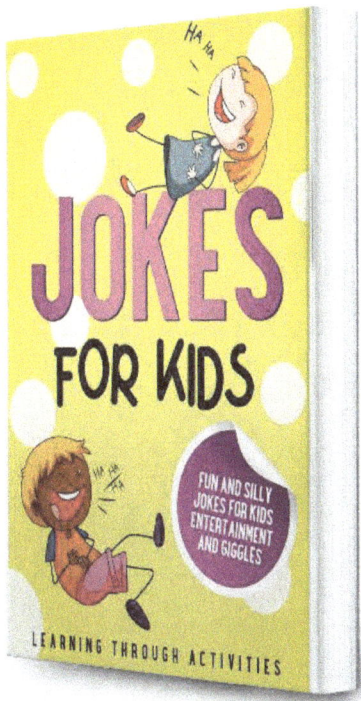

Get **FREE**, unlimited access to these and all of our new kids books by joining our community!

  Scan W/ Your Camera To Join!

www.ingramcontent.com/pod-product-compliance
Lightning Source LLC
Chambersburg PA
CBHW081627100526
44590CB00021B/3635